Contents

UNIT 1

Why Chartism?

The Tolpuddle Martyrs were six Dorset farm labourers who were sentenced to be transported to Australia for swearing an oath when joining a trade union in 1834. This huge demonstration in Copenhagen Fields, North London, took place on 21 April 1834 to protest against the sentence. In 1836 the men were pardoned and allowed to return.

In 1836 many people were unhappy at the way Britain was governed. There was a wide difference in the lives of the rich and poor. A number of **Radicals** had been demanding change ever since the end of the wars against France (1793–1815). Their efforts had been unsuccessful. The vast majority of the population was still unable to vote for the government and Members of Parliament who made the laws which controlled people's lives. Many of the working population, both in towns and in the countryside, lived in crowded, unsanitary slums. Their working conditions were bad and wages low. Many poor people had to decide between starvation or the workhouse. The workhouse took away their freedom and was degrading. How had things come to be like this, and what could be done to change the situation?

Wages and prices

During the wars against France there were bad harvests and it was difficult to import corn. Bread, the basic food of the poor, became very expensive. Wages were going up because the war helped industry and farming, but prices were going up faster. As a result, people could not buy as much with their wages as before. When the wars ended in 1815, the situation got worse. There was a slump in industry and agriculture. Taxes were put on many goods. The government brought in the **Corn Laws** in 1815. These laws kept

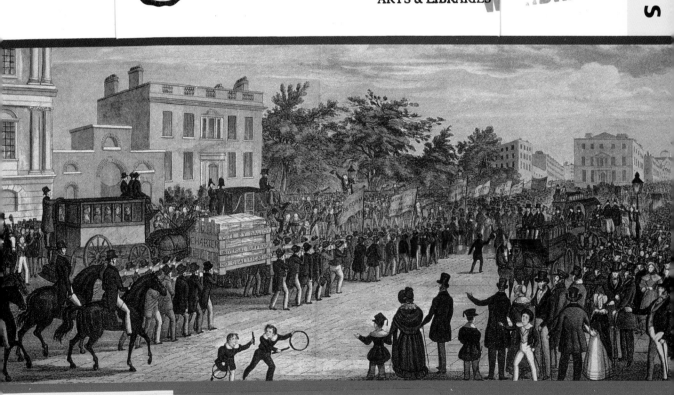

Bob Rees

Heinemann

Heinemann Educational,
a division of Heinemann Publishers (Oxford) Ltd,
Halley Court, Jordan Hill, Oxford OX2 8EJ

OXFORD LONDON EDINBURGH MADRID
ATHENS BOLOGNA PARIS MELBOURNE
SYDNEY AUCKLAND SINGAPORE TOKYO
IBADAN NAIROBI HARARE GABORONE
PORTSMOUTH NH (USA)

First published 1995

98 97 96 95 10 9 8 7 6 5 4 3 2 1

**British Library Cataloguing Data is available
from the British Library on request.**

ISBN 0 435 309315

Designed by Ron Kamen, Green Door Design Ltd,
Basingstoke

Illustrated by Douglas Hall

Printed in Spain by Mateu Cromo

The front cover shows the Chartists carrying the
1842 petition to Parliament.

Acknowledgements

The author and publisher would like to thank the
following for permission to reproduce photographs:

E.T. Archive: 1.1, 1.3, 4.5
Mary Evans Picture Libray: 3.4, 4.7, 5.1
Greater London Council: 3.7
Her Majesty the Queen: 4.13
Hulton Deutsch Collection: 4.1
Mansell Collection: 2.2, 5.4
Punch Library: 3.3, 4.8, 5.2, 5.5
Martin Sookias: 4.10
Weidenfeld and Nicolson Ltd: Cover and 4.12

Every effort has been made to contact copyright
holders of material published in this book. Any
omissions will be rectified in subsequent printings if
notice is given to the publisher.

Details of written sources

In some sources the wording or sentence structure
has been simplified to ensure that the source is
accessible.

A History of the Black Presence in London, Greater
London Council, 1986: 3.6
T. Charles-Edwards and B. Richardson, *They Saw it
Happen 1689-1897*, Basil Blackwell, 1958: 5.3
C. Culpin, *Expansion, Trade and Industry*, Collins
Educational; 1993: 2.3
K. Dawson and P. Wall, *Parliamentary Representation*,
OUP, 1968: 5.6
J. Epstein, *The Lion of Freedom*, Croom Helm, 1982:
2.6
C. McNab and R. Mackenzie, *From Waterloo to the
Great Exhibition*, Oliver and Boyd, 1982: 2.5, 4.11
B. O'Callaghan, *The Chartists*, Longman, 1974: 2.7
SCHP, *Britain 1815-51*, Holmes McDougall, 1977: 4.6
D. Thompson, *The Chartists*, Wildwood House, 1986:
2.4, 3.1, 3.2, 3.5, 4.2, 4.3, 4.9

> **Note**
>
> In this book some of the words are printed in **bold**
> type. This indicates that the word is listed in the
> glossary on page 31. The glossary gives a brief
> explanation of words that may be new to you.

SOURCE 2

The workhouse built at Andover in Hampshire. One side was for men and the other side was for women. In 1846 the Andover workhouse was the centre of a scandal when it was discovered that the inmates gnawed the rotting gristle on old bones that they were breaking up as fertilizer because the overseer gave them so little food.

QUESTIONS

1   Study Source 1. What does it tell you about Britain in 1834?

2   Using Source 2 and your own knowledge about this period, say what the following would probably have thought about the Andover workhouse :

a an inmate

b a Radical

c a farm worker.

the price of imported corn high. This helped the rich landowners but increased the problems of the poor. Many working people blamed the introduction of machinery for the loss of jobs. Some workers tried to improve their conditions by joining together in trade unions. These had been banned in 1799 but were allowed again in 1824. Most employers and the government were determined to stop the trade unions. They used harsh laws to punish union members. The most notorious case was that of the Tolpuddle Martyrs in 1834 (see Source 1). Trade Unions collapsed after this. Working people began to look for another way of improving their conditions.

The New Poor Law

Harsh conditions for the poor continued throughout the 1820s. Parishes were responsible for looking after the poor. Poor people, often called paupers, were given money to enable them to live at the most basic level. One way of helping the poor who had a job was called the Allowance System. People were given an amount of money by the parish to add to their wages. The amount given depended on the number of children in a family and the price of bread. By 1830, with the price of bread very high, rising unemployment and the population increasing, the Old Poor Law had become very expensive. In 1834, Parliament passed the **Poor Law Amendment Act**. This New Poor Law said that parishes, or groups of parishes called unions, must set up workhouses (see Source 2) where the poor would be kept. This system was cheaper, but it was bitterly resented by most of the poor. Families were separated, food was basic and the work was hard. Most of all, the poor hated losing their freedom.

In 1819, a Radical meeting at St Peter's Fields, Manchester, was attacked by soldiers after magistrates ordered them to break it up. Eleven of the unarmed crowd were killed and hundreds were injured. The attack was called 'Peterloo' after the battle of Waterloo, which ended the long war against Napoleonic France.

Calls for Reform

In 1815, Parliament was controlled by rich and powerful landowners. They were able to protect their own interests because they had no opposition. Only those who owned property were allowed to vote (about three per cent of the male population). In elections, bribery and vote-buying was widespread. Action to change this situation increased at the end of the French wars.

The middle class wanted to have a say in the running of the country because they were making money and paying taxes on goods. Others, including Radicals such as Henry Hunt and William Cobbett, wanted the vote for working-class people. Sometimes their protests turned into riots such as those at Spa Fields, London in 1816 and St Peter's Fields, Manchester in 1819. The government struck back by using armed force and passing laws like the **Six Acts**, in 1819, to try to stop calls for the reform of Parliament.

THE LYING WHIG REFORM BILL,

THE FOLLOWING TABLES EXHIBIT THE MONSTROUS DELUSION THAT THE REFORM BILL DESTROYED THE ROTTEN BOROUGH SYSTEM.

1.—Contested Elections, 1837, and subsequently, at which the votes polled for a successful candidate were less than 200.

	BOROUGH OR COUNTY.	RETURNS	POLLED	CONSTITUENCY FROM WHOM FORMED.	POPULATION.
1	Ashburton	1	98	101 nom. freem. &342 h.	4,165
2	Arundel	1	176	380 £10 h.	2,803
3	Banbury	1	185	old cor. of 18 & 365 h.	5,906
4	Bandon (Ireland)	1	133	13 f. and 279 h.	9,820
5	Brecon	1	151	350 h.	5,026
6	Caithnesshire	1	198	. . . . .	34,000
7	Carlow (Ireland)	1	167	23 f. and 403 h.	9,012
8	Cockermouth	2	117	burghage holders &235h.	6,022
9	Colerain (Ireland)	1	129	52 f. and 240 h.	5,752
10	Devizes	2	109	cor. and 409 h.	6,367
11	Downpatrick (I.)	1	190		4,779
12	Eversham	2	168	130 h.	3,991
13	Frome	1	125	450 h.	12,240
14	Harwich	1	75	cor. and 202 h.	4,297
15	Helston	1	160	cor. and 225 h.	3,293
16	Horsham	1	147	burghage tenants & 365h	5,105
17	Kidderminster	1	198	500 h.	20,165
18	Kinsale (Ireland)	1	102	301 h.	6,897
19	Knaresborough	2	172	burghage tenants&369h	6,252
20	Liskeard	1	113	cor. and 315 h.	4,042
21	Ludlow	2	194	b. and 314 h.	5,252
22	Lyme Regis	1	121	f. and 300 h.	3,345
23	Lymington	2	161	cor. and 189 h.	5,472
24	Petersfield	1	125	freeh. and 305 h.	4,922
25	Sligo (Ireland)	1	178	13 f. and 680 h.	12,762
26	Totness	2	158	f. and 316 h.	3,442
27	Tralee (Ireland)	1	75	13 f. and 354 h.	9,562
28	Wallingford	1	159	cor. and 278 h.	2,467
29	Wareham	1	170	s. and c. and 54 h.	2,566
30	Woodstock	1	126	f. and 373 h.	7,055
31	Youghal (Ireland)	1	158	f. and 479 h.	9,600

2.—Contested Elections, and voters polled under 300.

	BOROUGH OR COUNTY.	RETURNS	POLLED	CONSTITUENCY FROM WHOM FORMED.	POPULATION.
1	Armagh (Ireland)	1	235	13 f. and 520 h.	9,189
2	Ashton-under-Lyne	1	234	610 h.	14,673
3	Banffshire	1	292		48,000
4	Bodmin	1	200	c. and 311 h.	5,228
5	Bridport	2	283	s. and l., and 342 h.	4,242
6	Buckingham	2	235	c. and 225 h.	3,610
7	Bury	1	248	765 h.	15,086
8	Bury St. Edmunds	2	289	719	11,436
9	Clonmell (Ireland)	1	284	94 f. and 752 h.	12,256
10	Gateshead	1	266	750 h.	15,177
11	Guildford	2	252	f. and 431 h.	3,916
12	Haddingshire	1	299		36,100
13	Ditto Districts	1	268	214 h.	. . . .
14	Haverfordwest do.	1	247	s. and l., and 584 h.	10,832
15	Honiton	2	294	s. and l., and 318 h.	3,509
16	Hythe	1	243	f. and 537 h.	6,903
17	Inverness-shire	1	254		94,800
18	Kirkaldy Burghs	1	216		. . . .
19	Londonderry (I.)	1	214	f. and 735 h.	14,020
20	Newport (I. of W.)	2	264	f. and 445 h.	6,786
21	Peeblesshire	1	251		10,600
22	Poole	2	272	f. and 296 h.	6,959
23	Scarborough	2	225	c. and 508 h.	8,760
24	Selkirkshire	1	230		6,800
25	Shaftesbury	1	221	s. and l., and 145 h.	8,518
26	St. Albans	2	252	s. and l., and 286 h.	5,771
27	St. Andrews	1	290	452 h.	. . . .
28	Tewkesbury	2	219	f. and 262 h.	5,780
29	Teignmouth	1	259	1,150 h.	23,206
30	Warrington	1	278	973 h.	18,184
31	Weymouth	2	289	c. and 490 h.	8,095
32	Wigan	2	268	b. and 568 h.	20,774
33	Winchester	2	259	b. and 807 h.	9,212

NOTE.—*C., corporation; s. and l.. scot and lot voters; f., freeman; h., occupants of houses at an annual rental of £10 and upwards.*

The Reform Act, 1832

By 1830, some MPs were worried that a revolution might happen unless things were changed. After a struggle between the **Whig** and **Tory** parties, the **Reform Act** was passed in 1832. This gave MPs to some industrial cities like Manchester, but bribery remained because voting was still done by a show of hands. The right to vote still depended on the ownership of property, so most people were still excluded. Working people were bitterly disappointed because the Act did not give them the vote. They believed that only when the law allowed working people to become MPs would their living conditions be improved. In 1838 the **London Working Men's Association** published six demands in a document called the **People's Charter** (see page 8). Those who supported these demands were known as **Chartists** and their movement was called **Chartism.**

This Chartist newspaper, **The Poor Man's Guardian**, claimed that in 1837, five years after the Reform Act, MPs were still being elected by very small numbers of voters, even though the Act was supposed to get rid of 'rotten boroughs' (places that had an MP but very few voters).

ACTIVITIES

1 Describe what is happening in Source 3. How reliable do you think Source 3 might be?

2 What were the Chartists hoping to achieve by the newspaper article in Source 4?

3 Using the sources, the information in the text and your own knowledge, write a letter to a newspaper. It should be from a Chartist to say why change was necessary.

SOURCE 1

The Six Points
OF THE
PEOPLE'S
CHARTER.

1. A VOTE for every man twenty-one years of age, of sound mind, and not undergoing punishment for crime.

2. THE BALLOT.—To protect the elector in the exercise of his vote.

3. No PROPERTY QUALIFICATION for Members of Parliament —thus enabling the constituencies to return the man of their choice, be he rich or poor.

4. PAYMENT OF MEMBERS, thus enabling an honest trades-man, working man, or other person, to serve a constituency, when taken from his business to attend to the interests of the country.

5. EQUAL CONSTITUENCIES, securing the same amount of representation for the same number of electors, instead of allowing small constituencies to swamp the votes of large ones.

6. ANNUAL PARLIAMENTS, thus presenting the most effectual check to bribery and intimidation, since though a constituency might be bought once in seven years (even with the ballot), no purse could buy a constituency (under a system of universal suffrage) in each ensuing twelvemonth; and since members, when elected for a year only, would not be able to defy and betray their constituents as now.

This handbill, published in 1838, set out the Six Points of the People's Charter. First drawn up by William Lovett of the London Working Men's Association, the Charter was presented to Parliament by Thomas Attwood, leader of the Birmingham Political Union. The Six Points grew out of feelings of disappointment with the 1832 Reform Act, anger at the New Poor Law and misery at the lack of employment in the 1830s. Handbills like this were an important way of spreading information at a time when communications were often slow, expensive and difficult.

All Chartists believed in the Six Points of the People's Charter. The heart of Chartist beliefs was that the vote was a basic right which should be shared by all men. Chartists wanted the ballot, so that people could vote in secret without being threatened by opponents. They did not want the property qualification because it stopped poor people standing for parliament. Payment of Members would allow working people to become MPs. Equal constituencies (voting areas) would mean that everyone would be fairly represented. To avoid bribery annual parliaments, with an election each year, would make it too costly to buy people's votes.

Apart from this, however, Chartists disagreed about other things they wanted. For example, some Chartist groups wanted working hours cut to eight per day. Others wanted the Poor Law Amendment Act done away with. Many Chartists wanted better education for working people. Chartists were also divided about the methods they should use. These divisions grew deeper as time went on.

Moral force Chartists

The person who wrote the People's Charter, William Lovett, was the leader of the moral force Chartists. They believed that education, reason and persuasion would achieve their aims.

Moral force Chartists believed that the working class should join with the middle class to remove the power of the landowners and Tories. Many Chartist leaders, especially at a local level, followed the ideas of Lovett. One of their main ideas was to present petitions to Parliament so that their demands could be discussed. This approach was also favoured by Thomas Attwood, the leader of the Birmingham Political Union. Attwood presented the first Chartist petition to Parliament in 1839. Two more were presented in 1842 and 1848 (see pages 23–24).

Physical force Chartists

Other Chartists had no faith in the idea of a partnership with the middle classes. They believed that employers wanted to increase their power and wanted the New Poor Law not only to keep down the money they had to pay for the poor rates, but also to drive down wages. They felt that employers wanted to make working people work long hours for low wages. Physical force Chartists believed that they could get their demands only by force – by armed uprising. A few believed that violent revolution was necessary if the condition of the working class was to be improved. An Irishman called Feargus O'Connor, who became the national leader of the Chartists, was one of those who believed in physical force. Another supporter of physical force was George Julian Harney.

Christian Chartism

During the first half of the 19th century many Church of England ministers looked down upon poor people. They told them that God had made them poor and they should not complain if they wanted to go to Heaven. The **Methodists** were more sympathetic to the poor. Even so, some Methodist ministers warned their congregations against Chartism. They said the Chartists were wrong to hold meetings in public houses and give political speeches on a Sunday.

However, many Chartists were keen Christians and wanted to go to church. In many areas, therefore, Chartists set up their own churches. Here they worshipped and listened to sermons which put over the Chartist message. The Christian Chartists believed that the inequalities between rich and poor needed to be removed. The most famous Christian Chartist was Arthur O'Neil, founder of the Birmingham Chartist Church.

Chartists had a wide range of interests and demands throughout their history.

Some Chartist meetings were held in taverns. Cartoons like this one, drawn by George Cruikshank, were used by the opponents of Chartism to make fun of what they thought might happen if the Chartists got into Parliament. Why would opponents of Chartism want a cartoon like this published?

Temperance Chartists

Some Chartist groups held their meetings in public houses, and their opponents were able to ridicule their meetings as drunken parties (see Source 2). Some Chartists thought that drink was a problem for the working class. They said it stopped working people from improving their education and took away their self-respect. Temperance Chartists, therefore, said that alcohol should be avoided.

The idea of temperance reform was also popular among religious people and the middle classes. The temperance Chartists' beliefs were often slightly different. While they condemned drunkenness, they saw temperance as a way to get political power by showing that working people were very capable of clean living and good behaviour.

Knowledge Chartists

For some Chartists, their movement was an opportunity to improve the education of the working class. Many Chartist societies held classes for the 'self-improvement' of the workers. Visiting lecturers spoke on a wide variety of topics. In Manchester, in 1840, the factory owners advised their workers that they must get an education before they could have any claim to the right to vote. Visiting lecturers were also popular in the villages of Wiltshire. In some areas Chartists set up their own schools. The moral force Chartists were the most enthusiastic supporters of education. When Chartism suffered setbacks in its demands for political reform, they saw workers' education as a reason to continue the movement.

SOURCE 3

Let us, Friends, join together the honest, moral, hard-working and thinking members of society. Let us obtain a library of books. Let us publish our views so that we create a moral, thinking, energetic force in politics.

An extract from a speech made by William Lovett in 1838. Lovett wanted Parliament to see that working-class people deserved to have their demands listened to and be given the vote.

SOURCE 4

A politician in Leeds who used to visit public houses to discuss politics was interrupted by his wife entering. She suggested that he should take his money home to her and his starving children, making his home more comfortable – rather than finding fault with Lord John Russell, the Prime Minister.

*Benjamin Wilson, writing in his memoirs, **The Struggles of an Old Chartist**, 1887, about events in 1847.*

SOURCE 5

Shall it be said that four million men, capable of bearing arms, allowed a few oppressors at home to enslave and degrade them? We have said we will get our rights by peace if we can but we will use force if we have to. Beware those who begin the fight with the masses or who resist their call for justice.

*Feargus O'Connor put forward his point of view in his newspaper, the **Northern Star** in July 1847.*

SOURCE 6

I am convinced that the real practical work now is the forming of societies in various towns for building halls in which members may improve their political, religious and scientific knowledge.

Henry Vincent, a well-known Chartist leader, wrote this while in prison in 1840. He was writing to Francis Place who was another well-known supporter of reform.

SOURCE 7

Cannon balls may aid the truth
But thought's a weapon stronger
We'll win our battle by its aid –
Wait a little longer.

A verse from a popular Chartist song.

ACTIVITIES

1   What were the differences between moral force and physical force Chartists?

2   Explain the ideas of these Chartist groups:
    • **Christian Chartists**
    • **Temperance Chartists**
    • **Knowledge Chartists**

3   For each of Sources 3 to 7 say which group of Chartists they come from. Explain your decisions.

4   What did all Chartists have in common?

Who were the Chartists?

Chartism appealed to many different people. In most Chartist groups there were four types of members:

- Radical reformers who worked full-time organizing political protests. These people provided the leaders of the Chartist movement.

- Young people who were caught up by the enthusiasm of Chartism.

- Loyal supporters, who were eager to sign petitions, to attend meetings and also to take part in the social activities of Chartism, such as processions, education classes and Chartist church services.

- People who tended to be rather fickle. Sometimes they were enthusiastic, but they lost their interest if things went badly for the movement.

Each group was made up of different sections of society. There were ordinary workers, trades people and shopkeepers, clergymen and professional people, and middle-class Radicals.

Personality clashes meant that leaders like O'Connor and Lovett came to hate each other. Lovett called O'Connor 'The Big I Am of politics' because the Irishman wanted to be seen as the single leader of the movement and could not accept disagreement with his views.

The divisions in the Chartist movement can be seen in the number of groups set up to represent different Chartists. The **National Chartist Association** was founded by O'Connor in July 1840. Joseph Sturge helped found the **Complete Suffrage Union** in 1842 which aimed to unite Chartists and the middle-class Radicals.

WE WANT THE PEOPLE'S CHARTER

Chartists came from all groups in society. Women, workers, employers, traders, lawyers and journalists joined with politicians to put forward their demand for the right to vote.

Women and Chartism

Women were important in the Chartist movement. In Birmingham, 24,000 women signed the first petition in 1839. At its height the Chartist movement involved whole communities. Entire families shared hopes and took action. Women took part in meetings, processions, social events, classes and riots. Many Chartists saw the perhaps obvious point that the country was ruled by a woman, Queen Victoria, yet women had no political rights.

William Lovett claimed that his first draft of the Charter contained a demand for votes for women, but that this was dropped because some thought it would harm the chances of getting votes for men. One person who supported votes for women was Charles Neesom. His wife, Elizabeth, became the leading woman Chartist in London. Women's groups featured throughout the country. When Henry Vincent 'introduced' the Charter in Bath in 1838, at least half his audience were women. Many female Radical associations were set up. In the North, women were particularly angry about the New Poor Law. In the village of Elland, near Halifax, the Radical women met Thomas Power, a **Poor Law Commissioner**, and 'rolled him in the snow'. In 1840, Martha Holmes was jailed for assaulting an ex-Chartist who had become a police informer.

THINK IT THROUGH

Miss Ruthwell (Source 1) and Jane Jones (Source 2) had different ideas about Chartism. What were the differences? Why were they different?

SOURCE 1

Three cheers were given when Miss Ruthwell arrived. She said that she was aware that some people might think that she was a 'bold and forward girl' because she was speaking to a meeting of hundreds of intelligent men. That was because society had created such ideas. If her family had not been badly treated and if she, her brother and her sister had not been sacked for going to a meeting about improving the conditions of Power Loom Weavers, then she would still have been slaving at her job. She would never have even thought why things were so bad. Now the time was coming when the weavers would rise above their slavery and the cruelty of the employers would end for ever. While she had a voice to speak about the wrongs done to working women, while she had a drop of British blood in her veins, she would work for the freedom of her class and the female workers of Bradford would be a powerful force in the struggle for 'a fair day's wage for a fair day's work'. She was loudly cheered when she finished.

Miss Ruthwell was the treasurer of the Bradford Power Loom Weavers' Society. She was one of the few women Chartists to leave an account of her life. This report of one of her speeches was in the Northern Star, 9 May 1845.

SOURCE 2

Better to be the wife of a wandering peddler – at least we could tramp about together, carrying our children on our backs, and enjoy each other's company – than be the wife of a travelling Chartist lecturer.

Mrs Jane Jones wrote this letter to her husband, the Chartist leader Ernest Jones, in 1851. He suffered for being a Chartist. His wife shared the hardships, but not his political beliefs.

HOW TO TREAT THE FEMALE CHARTISTS.

*This cartoon was printed in the magazine **Punch** in 1848. The magazine said that London was threatened by female Chartists. George Sand was a popular woman novelist.*

In Nottingham, Birmingham, Bradford, Lancashire and Scotland, as well as other places, women's groups played prominent parts in Chartist activities. In Ashton-under-Lyne, a town where Chartism was strong, many young people were introduced to radical politics by the celebrations organized by women to commemorate the anniversary of Peterloo.

As well as demonstrating and making speeches, women supported the Chartist movement in other ways. One way was to name their children after leading Chartists. Nancy Brear of Birkenhead had her son baptised Henry Vincent O'Connor Brear. Other women set up schools, in the words of Sarah Foden of Sheffield, 'to give their children the principles of Chartism'. Some women had to pay a high price for their involvement. As a result of a revolt in Sheffield in 1842, Mary Holberry's husband, Samuel, was put in prison where he died from the cruel treatment he received. Their baby son also died during that time.

Women's activity was at its height in the early years of Chartism. In 1839, Elizabeth Cresswell was imprisoned for carrying a pistol at a demonstration in Mansfield. At Llanidloes, in Wales, three women were jailed for their part in a riot. Amy Meredith was arrested for stealing a gun to take part in the Newport rising of 1839 (see page 19). As demonstrations against the New Poor Law lessened in the later 1840s, records of women's involvement decrease. But some women were active throughout Chartism's history.

QUESTIONS

1   **In what ways did women support Chartism?**

2   **Study Source 3. How is *Punch* suggesting that women Chartists should be resisted? Do you think *Punch* supported female Chartism? Explain your decisions.**

This engraving shows the Chartist meeting on Kennington Common in 1848. The meeting was held before the delivery of the Chartists' third petition to Parliament.

Workers, artisans and tradespeople

Chartism united varied groups of the working class, including industrial workers, miners and farm workers. They were joined by skilled craftspeople, shopkeepers, professional people and middle-class Radicals.

Some farm workers were Chartists, although there are few records of them being leaders. The case of the Tolpuddle Martyrs (see pages 4–5) helps to explain why Chartism started. Some landowners tried hard to stop their labourers from getting involved. In 1839, a magistrate from Trowbridge, Wiltshire, wrote in panic to the Home Secretary that his own gardeners had joined the Working Men's Association. A local farmer sacked all the workers who had joined. At Friston, Norfolk, in 1838 a landowner gave a feast for his workers to keep them from a Chartist rally. Another farmer bribed his farmhands with a large sack of potatoes each.

SOURCE 5

If farmers think there is nothing to be feared from the farm workers, they are mistaken. I do not believe there is any village near me that would not be ready to take, by brute force, the rewards of their own labour. Every parish is ready for any outbreak.

*Elliot Yorke, MP for Cambridgeshire, warns farmers about letting their workers listen to visiting Chartists from the towns. From the **Cambridgeshire Chronicle, March 1846.***

Shoemakers were a particularly active group in Chartism. Thomas Cooper, the famous Chartist leader from Leicester, was one. Chartism was popular among textile workers. Both factory hands and outworkers, like handloom weavers, followed Chartism. Blacksmiths were important among Chartists because they often made the weapons used in riots, and used their physical strength against the authorities. When Isaac Jefferson of Bingley, Yorkshire, was arrested in 1848, his wrists were too large for the police handcuffs to fit. The miners were the shock troops of the Chartist movement, inspiring fear among the 'respectable' classes.

One tailor who became an important Chartist leader was William Cuffay, a member of Britain's Black community. He held many important positions and, in 1848, organized the procession to present the third petition to Parliament.

The reasons why these people joined the Chartists were varied. Many craftspeople were worried about losing their jobs because of new machines. In the industrial areas of Northern England, Scotland and South Wales workers became interested in Chartism when trade depressions brought unemployment.

SOURCE 7

William Cuffay (1788–1870) was born at Chatham in Kent. His father had been a slave in the West Indies. In 1848, Cuffay was found guilty of plotting to set fire to buildings in London. He was transported to Tasmania, where he died in the workhouse.

SOURCE 6

He was transported because the government was afraid of him. Whilst honesty and honour are admired the name of William Cuffay, a son of Africa's downtrodden people, will always be remembered.

A contemporary opinion about Cuffay in Reynolds Political Register. This was a newspaper published by George Reynolds, a Chartist from Derby.

ACTIVITIES

1 Is Source 6 biased? Does this mean it will not be useful for studying the Chartist movement?

2 a What was the attitude of many landowners and farmers towards Chartism?
   b Why did they have such an attitude?

3 Look back over the whole unit.
   a Which people supported Chartism?
   b Why did Chartism appeal to so many different people?

What did the Chartists do?

Chartist centres

Chartism was a widespread movement. Chartist groups were formed in small towns such as Hadleigh in Essex as well as industrial cities like Leeds. Chartism found a ready audience in the industrial North where the New Poor Law hit working people hard. Chartism was swiftly accepted in traditionally Radical areas like Birmingham, London and Bristol. Where industrial changes were causing hardship such as the textile towns of Somerset and Wiltshire, places like Trowbridge became Chartist centres. Other Somerset towns like Shepton Mallet, Taunton and Wells have no records of Chartist activity.

Chartist meetings

Chartists were keen on meetings. Sometimes these were on a national level, like the Conventions at London and Birmingham in 1839. Locally, Chartist leaders and visiting lecturers gave speeches and held discussion groups. There were social events like tea parties and business meetings to elect representatives or collect funds.

SOURCE 1

The first Chartist Convention met in the British Coffee House, Cockspur Street, London, in February 1839. It called itself the General Convention of the Industrious Classes. In May 1839 it moved to Birmingham. Delegates came from all over Britain.

SOURCE 2

Manchester, Birmingham, Sheffield, Leeds and Glasgow had important manufacturing districts in them. London, Bristol and some of the older ports and cities had felt the effects of changes in industry less. However, all these places had Chartist groups of some size and saw conflict between the people and the authorities. The districts where the Chartists were in control for a time were the textile towns like Bradford, Halifax and Bolton, counties like Nottinghamshire and Leicestershire, and mining areas like South Wales and Newcastle.

*Dorothy Thompson, a modern historian, wrote this account of important Chartist centres in her book **The Chartists** in 1984.*

17

Some meetings were meant to stir up protest or violent action. For example, the Chartists of Bath wanted to hold a mass meeting on 20 May 1839. But 130 police, 600 special constables, a troop of Hussars and six troops of part-time soldiers were gathered by the magistrates to stop it. Desperate workers in northern industrial areas often turned to violence and riot to achieve their aims.

Most meetings were less dramatic. Henry Vincent, released from jail on 31 January 1841, gave two lectures in Bath on democratic government, sobriety and unity. Charles Bolwell toured south Wiltshire in April, and McDouall, a national figure, spoke in Trowbridge. Mr Clewer, a 'professional teetotaller' lectured in Bradford on Avon, Melksham and Trowbridge. Chartists often bought their own premises, called 'rooms' or 'Democratic Chapels'. They also hired halls or met in the home of one of their members.

SOURCE 3

It was a very different affair to the later meetings of Mr O'Connor's travelling lecturers. There were lawyers, clergymen, merchants, members of my own profession, writers and a large number of honest and intelligent working men.

The first Chartist Convention in 1839, described in a letter by Matthew Fletcher, a Radical surgeon and one of the delegates.

SOURCE 4

To The Poor of Bath

On Monday next a Meeting is to be held to consider the relief of your sufferings. The object of the meeting is, doubtless, most laudable. Will it remove THE CAUSE of your distress? NO! CHARITY will be extended to a small degree, but JUSTICE WILL BE DENIED. You have to pay the Queen every year £300,000; Prince Albert £30,000; AND MANY MILLIONS MORE ARE EXTORTED FROM YOU. To pay this everything you hear, see, feel or taste is taxed. IF A POOR MAN EARNS ONE POUND, FIFTEEN SHILLINGS ARE TAKEN IN TAXES!
SUFFERERS – It is time THE SYSTEM should be changed. Attend the meeting in thousands. Come in your rags and tatters. Be there at the appointed time – be peaceful, behave respectful – but do not leave until your wrongs are proclaimed. YOU MUST HAVE THE POWER OF ELECTING REPRESENTATIVES TO PROTECT YOU FROM THE OPPRESSION OF THE EXCLUSIVE REPRESENTATION OF THE WEALTHY CLASSES.

This poster was issued in Bath on 9 January 1841. Posters like this were an important way in which the Chartists could spread news of their activities. Newspapers were expensive due to the tax charged by the government.

Chartist violence

The violent actions of some Chartists terrified many. In November 1839, 5,000 miners and ironworkers marched on the town of Newport in South Wales. They were led by John Frost, ex-mayor of Newport. They decided to take over the town of Newport and release the Chartists imprisoned there, including Henry Vincent. The Chartists marched on the Westgate Hotel. The magistrates were warned and soldiers fired into the crowd. Up to twenty people were killed. The leaders of the revolt were sentenced to transportation for life to Australia.

SOURCE 5

The Newport rising, 1839. This contemporary print shows the Chartist crowd firing on the soldiers in the Westgate Hotel. The leaders were John Frost, William Jones and Zephenia Williams. The crowd ran when the soldiers fired.

SOURCE 6

A company of the 45th Regiment was stationed at the Westgate Hotel. The crowd marched there, cheering loudly. When they arrived there, they attacked. The magistrates and police were driven from the streets and ran in the hotel for safety. The soldiers were at the windows and some people began to fire at them. The soldiers, of course, fired back. The result was that, in about twenty minutes, ten Chartists were killed on the spot and about fifty others were wounded.

Reginald Gammage was a lifelong Chartist. He wrote this description of the Newport rising in **The History of the Chartist Movement,** *published in 1855.*

QUESTIONS

1   **In what ways does Source 6 agree with Source 5? In what ways does it disagree?**

2   **How would you work out whether Source 6 was reliable?**

This riot took place in Stockport, Lancashire, in 1842. Chartists broke into the local workhouse, or 'bastille', and distributed the food that they found there. Later, they burnt the building down.

Sometimes reports of Chartist violence were exaggerated by newspapers, particularly O'Connor's *Northern Star*. Lurid reports, in 1848, of cavalry charges on mass gatherings in Glasgow, bread riots and all-night fighting at barricades astonished the Chartists of the city. However, there were outbreaks of rioting in many areas. Police from London fought with Chartists in the Bull Ring riots in Birmingham in July 1839. There was also fighting at Sheffield, Bradford and Dewsbury. Rioters were shot dead at Preston in 1842.

The 1834 Poor Law provoked a number of riots. The hated **bastilles**, as the workhouses were called, became a focus of mob action. Sometimes, as at Stockport in 1842, rioters broke into the workhouses to take bread.

THINK IT THROUGH

Does Source 7 mean that the Chartists were against the poor?

SOURCE 8

*This cartoon was published in **Punch** in 1848. It claims to show 'A Physical Force Chartist Arming for the Fight'.*

SOURCE 9

The sight was impossible to forget. They came down the road in thousands. A gaunt, hungry looking, desperate crowd armed with huge clubs, pitchforks, and pikes. Many didn't have coat and hats. Hundreds and hundreds had their clothes in rags and tatters. Most were full of wild excitement.

*Frank Peel describes the march of Chartist strikers from Bradford to Halifax in 1842. His book, **Rising of the Luddites, Chartists and Plug-drawers**, was published in 1880.*

Strikes

Strikes were always seen by many Chartists as a weapon for achieving their aims. At the first Chartist Convention in 1839, the differences between the moral force and the physical force Chartists were not settled, but it was decided to hold a general strike, often called the Sacred Month or the National Holiday. The strike was a failure and it was called off after a week.

In 1842, industrial depression caused many factory workers in the North of England to be thrown out of work. Employers cut wages. There were numerous strikes. Thomas Cooper, a Chartist leader, said that the strikes should continue 'until the People's Charter became the law of the Land'. Some strikers took the plugs out of the boilers of the steam engines that powered factory machines, so that they could not work. These strikes became known as the Plug Plots. Soldiers were sent to guard the factories and the strikers soon returned to work.

THINK IT THROUGH

Is Source 8 in favour of physical force Chartism?

Does Source 9 have the same opinion of physical force Chartism as Source 8? Why might they be different?

This building was the school at Snig's End, a Chartist village set up in what is now Gloucestershire, in June 1847. This was part of the Chartist Land Plan. Among the settlers there was a blacksmith from Wells, in Somerset, and a carpenter from London.

The Chartist Land Plan

Feargus O'Connor came up with many plans during his career. When the 1842 petition was rejected by Parliament, he turned to an idea designed to improve the lives of working people. By creating special Chartist communities, workers could live on their own property and achieve a dignity and quality of life that they could not get in the squalid slums where most of them lived. The idea was that people would escape the harsh drudgery of the factories, and live by growing their own food and supporting each other. Five communities were set up and workers, both agricultural and industrial, bought shares in O'Connor's Chartist Land Company to get a plot of land. One village, near Watford, was called O'Connorville in honour of its founder. O'Connor promoted the idea by promising wonderful crops, but he knew little about farming and the company was badly run. A government inquiry found that O'Connor had mismanaged the company and most settlers had to leave. The company ended in 1851.

Every acre was to grow on average such crops as no acre ever grew, except under the rarest combination of good climate, great skill and unlimited manure. Every cow was to live forever, and give more milk than any except the best cows ever gave before. They would never be dry. Every pig was to be the best and every goose was to be a swan.

*This description of what the Chartist Land Company's settlements were supposed to be like was printed in the **Edinburgh Review**. When O'Connor opened these settlements, he sometimes waved giant cabbages about to show his aims.*

QUESTIONS

1   What was the Chartist Land Plan?

2   Why did O'Connor set it up?

3   What impression of the Chartist Land Plan do you get from Sources 10 and 11?

4   Why did the Chartists Land Plan fail?

Chartist petitions

The Chartists presented three petitions in 1839, 1842 and 1848 designed to get Parliament to accept the demands of the People's Charter. The petitions were always presented following a period of high prices, unemployment and poverty. Support for Chartism increased at times like this.

The first petition, 1839

The Convention which met in both London and Birmingham in 1839 managed to get 1,283,000 people to sign the demand that Parliament grant the People's Charter. The presentation of the signatures caused problems. Delays were caused by arguments between the moral and physical force groups.

Then the government resigned, so the petition was further held up. Finally, in May 1839, the petition was taken to Parliament, where it was put to the vote by Thomas Attwood and John Fielden. It was rejected by a vote of 235 to 46. The rejection of the petition led to violence, including the Sacred Month (see page 21) and the Newport rising, and the arrest and imprisonment of Chartist leaders including William Lovett and Feargus O'Connor.

The second petition, 1842

In 1842, when poverty and hunger were widespread in industrial areas, the Chartists put forward their second petition. This time they had over three and a quarter million signatures. Perhaps the Trowbridge Chartist who said that what people really wanted was 'plenty of roast beef, plum pudding and strong beer' was accurate. It took 50 men to carry the signatures into Parliament, where Thomas Duncombe presented it. It was rejected by a vote of 287 to 49. The Plug Plots followed. Lovett was disgusted by the violence. He even left the movement for a time saying that 'violent words do not slay the enemies, but the friends of our movement.'

SOURCE *12*

The Chartist petition of 1842 was accompanied by a huge crowd. The beginning of the petition demanded the end of the Poor Law Amendment Act and of the Union of Britain with Ireland. This meant that Parliament was bound to reject it.

This is one of the earliest photographs ever taken. It shows the 1848 meeting on Kennington Common before the third petition.

The third petition, 1848

The final petition took place in 1848. Again, hard times had returned to harm the working class. The Chartists were also inspired by the revolutions taking place in several European countries. O'Connor was now MP for Nottingham. The delivery of the petition was preceded by a meeting on Kennington Common. The idea was that a crowd of 500,000 would march on Parliament and demand that the Charter was accepted.

The meeting took place but only about 20,000 turned up. The government was very worried and the Duke of Wellington was instructed to prepare troops and police to resist the expected riot. Over 150,000 special constables were enrolled, including Isambard Kingdom Brunel the famous railway builder and engineer. After a panic that O'Connor had been arrested when he went to negotiate with the police leader, the crowd left quietly and the expected trouble did not take place. However, there was some disorder and looting later.

ACTIVITIES

1 Compare Source 12 with Source 9. How do they give different impressions of Chartist activity? Explain why this might be.

2 Study Source 4 on page 15. Now look at Source 13 above. Is Source 4 based on Source 13? How are they similar? How are they different?

3 Using the text, the sources and your own knowledge, create a display of posters called 'What the Chartists did'.

Did the Chartists fail?

The Bank of England in London was fortified against the Chartists in April 1848. This picture shows sandbags and special constables. Government employees were given rifles and troops of soldiers were on duty at the Bank.

Petitions

As we have seen, the 1839 and 1842 Chartist Petitions were both rejected by Parliament. Strikes and riots followed. The government ordered the arrest of hundreds of Chartists. Many middle-class people were frightened away from supporting Chartist ideas. Large-scale Chartist support died away because of this and the fact that unemployment and poverty temporarily decreased. The third and final petition, which took place in 1848, ended in chaos.

O'Connor wanted the meeting and march to Parliament to be peaceful. Some Chartists wanted something more violent. They expected the petition to be rejected and looked forward to a revolution in Britain. However, the crowd at Kennington was much smaller than expected. O'Connor was nervous and feeling ill. As he was about to start the meeting, he was stopped by Sir Richard Mayne, Metropolitan Police Commissioner, who told him that the procession would not be allowed to cross the river Thames. O'Connor backed down and asked the crowd to disperse. He said he would present the petition to Parliament. The crowd trudged home, soaked by a downpour of rain. The event has been called a 'fiasco' but, by backing down, O'Connor had probably prevented a lot of bloodshed.

*This cartoon appeared in **Punch** in 1848. It is a comment upon the discovery that many of the signatures on the third Chartist petition were forged. 'Pugnose' and 'Longnose' were two of the invented signatures.*

The petition was closely examined in the House of Commons. It was found that there were only 1,975,000 signatures instead of the 5,700,000 claimed. Even these included many obvious forgeries, such as the Duke of Wellington, Queen Victoria and the anti-Chartist MP Colonel Sibthorp. There were also silly names like 'No cheese', 'Cheeks the Marine' and 'Mr Punch'. As a result, the Charter was rejected for the third and last time by 222 votes to 17. There were some minor Chartist riots in London in the summer of 1848. The government continued to imprison Chartist leaders, including William Cuffay. By now the Chartist leadership was in total chaos. It is not true that 1848 saw the end of Chartism, but the movement was never the same again.

SOURCE 3

April 9th – All London is making preparations to meet a Chartist row tomorrow. I went to the police office with all my clerks and messengers and we were all sworn in as special constables. We have to spend all day at the office tomorrow and I have to send down all my guns. Colonel Harness, of the Railway Department, is our commander-in-chief. Every gentleman in London has become a constable and there is an organisation of some sort in every district.

Charles Cavendish Greville was Clerk to the Privy Council, part of the government. His diary described the events of April 1848.

THINK IT THROUGH

How does Source 1 show that the government was concerned about the Chartist threat?

What attitude does Source 2 show towards the Charter? Did everyone agree?

This drawing shows the disturbances that took place in New Cross, London, as troops were leaving to put down riots in the North in 1842. The growing railway system speeded up the movement of soldiers. The government sent them into areas where they could combat any attempts by the Chartists to encourage violent uprisings.

Opposition to violence

The government was determined to crush the violent Chartist outbursts. The authorities, such as magistrates, took all the steps in their power to punish violence.

In the days before there was a police force outside London, magistrates had the duty to enforce the law. In 1839 the Rural Police Act was passed so that there could be police forces in areas outside London. This was widely seen as a measure to control working people and Radical politics. Magistrates could also call upon the police from London, special constables who were recruited to counter any threat, the Yeomanry (a kind of volunteer cavalry force) and the regular army regiments. Lodged in local people's houses, their organization was often chaotic.

THINK IT THROUGH

What does Source 4 show us about some people's attitudes to the government's use of soldiers against Chartists?

Sir Charles Napier

When trouble flared in 1839, Colonel Sir Charles Napier was appointed as commander of the troops in the North. This was a very interesting appointment as Napier and his family were Radicals. He had been a speaker at the Bath Working Men's Association meeting in 1837. He believed that working people should be allowed to vote. However, he was determined not to allow an armed Chartist uprising.

Colonel Napier was also a humane man. He made sure that his troops put on displays of their firepower to show their strength. He also sent personal messages to Chartist leaders at Manchester to persuade them that a rising was doomed. Napier asked the magistrates not to break up one great meeting at Kersal Moor (near Manchester) so that his soldiers would not have to attack the crowd.

In 1848, the army was used against the Chartists again. Troops and artillery, under the Duke of Wellington, protected London from the threat of violence.

SOURCE 5

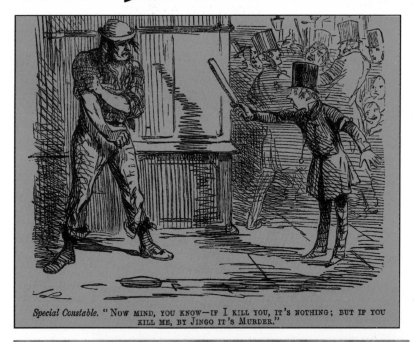

Special Constable. "NOW MIND, YOU KNOW—IF I KILL YOU, IT'S NOTHING; BUT IF YOU KILL ME, BY JINGO IT'S MURDER."

*This cartoon was published on 22 April 1848 in **Punch**. It shows a confrontation between a Chartist and a special constable.*

SOURCE 6

I am for a strong police, but the people should have the vote, the ballot, land to farm and education. England has many bad laws but should everyone arm themselves if they disagree with the law? The Poor cannot go on strike, they will rob and then they will be hanged. Physical force! Fools! What will they do when my cavalry is dancing around them and the cannons are pelting them? Poor men! How little they know of physical force!

Sir Charles Napier, commander of the northern garrisons of soldiers, wrote this letter to his brother, Sir William Napier, in 1839.

QUESTIONS

1   **Was *Punch* (Source 5) for or against the Chartists? Explain your answer.**

2   **Was Sir Charles Napier (Source 6) for or against the Chartists? Explain your answer.**

What happened to the Chartists?

After the failure of the 1848 petition Chartism slowly faded away. The working class lost interest and no longer supported the movement in large numbers. Why was this?

- The leadership of the movement was split. O'Connor and Lovett never agreed with each other. O'Connor also seemed to lose his nerve at vital moments, such as the 1848 meeting on Kennington Common.

- The government was quick to crush Chartist violence. Troops were sent to trouble spots and spies were used to inform the government of Chartist plans.

- Parliament was still controlled by landowners and farmers. They did not want to lose their powerful position by accepting the Charter.

- The Chartists lacked the money to run an effective publicity campaign. Middle-class people could have provided much needed money, but they were scared by the violence and did not support Chartism.

- After 1848 Britain entered a period of prosperity. Living standards improved. As we have already seen, people had little interest in Chartism when times were good.

- Working people turned to other ways of improving their lives. Some joined the new trade unions which were formed from 1851 onwards. Others joined the Co-operative Movement which provided food at reasonable prices and allowed members a share of the profits.

- Parliament began to pass a number of laws which helped the working class. The Corn Laws were abolished in 1846 and factory working hours were limited to ten per day in 1847.

O'Connor became more and more ill. In 1850, George Julian Harney took over the leadership of the movement. When O'Connor died, insane, in 1855, he was penniless. The Chartist Land Company was finished and his newspaper, the *Northern Star*, which had been so important in spreading Chartism, had been sold and shut down. The last Chartist Convention was held in 1858 and the movement was finally abandoned in 1860.

What happened to the Six Points?

The Chartists did not achieve any of the Six Points of the original People's Charter at the time. After 1860 the very name 'Chartist' was scarcely used. Yet some old Chartists lived to see some of their demands passed by later reforming parliaments. All of the points, except the unrealistic demand for a general election every year, have become law. The Chartists would be glad to know that their struggles were not in vain.

NO PROPERTY QUALIFICATIONS FOR MPs 1858

SECRET BALLOT 1872

EQUAL CONSTITUENCIES 1885

VOTES FOR MEN OVER 21 1918

PAYMENT FOR MPs 1911

ANNUAL ELECTIONS – *not achieved*

Eventually all the demands of the People's Charter were made law, except the one about annual elections.

ACTIVITIES

1 a What did the Chartists hope to achieve from the Kennington Common meeting?
  b Why did the meeting not have the intended result?

2 Why did Parliament reject the Third Petition?

3 How did the government deal with Chartist violence?

4 a Why did Chartism fade away after 1848?
  b Which of the reasons was the most important?
  c Was Chartism a total failure? Explain your answer.

Time Chart

1829   The Birmingham Political Union founded by Thomas Attwood.

1832   The Great Reform Act passed.

1836   London Working Men's Association founded by William Lovett.

1837   Working people complain about low wages and unemployment in places like Manchester, Nottingham, Yorkshire and Scotland (March).

          First edition of the *Northern Star*, the Chartist newspaper (November).

1838   The People's Charter first published in London. The National Petition first published in Birmingham.

1839   General Convention of the Industrious Classes held in London (February). The Convention moved to Birmingham (May). The Bull Ring riots took place in Birmingham. Many Chartists arrested (July).

          First National Petition rejected by the House of Commons (July).

          Newport Rising (November).

1840   Large scale Chartist arrests. Chartist Conference in Manchester. The National Charter Association formed (July).

1841   Tory Party won the General Election.

1842   Complete Suffrage Union Conference held in Birmingham followed by the Chartist Convention in London (April).

          Second National Petition rejected (May).

          Trade slump and unemployment (July).

          'Plug Plots' (August to September).

1843   Feargus O'Connor put on trial – acquitted of main charges.

1844   Chartist Convention met in Manchester (April).

1845   Chartist Convention met in London. Chartist Land Company formed by O'Connor.

1846   Corn Laws repealed (abolished).

1847   O'Connorville opened.

1848   Revolution in France (February). Third National Petition rejected (April). Many Chartists arrested (May and July).

1850   An argument between O'Connor and George Julian Harney resulted in Harney becoming the main Chartist leader.

1851   National Land Company closed.

1855   Death of O'Connor.

1858   Last Chartist Convention.

Glossary

bastilles French word meaning 'prison'. This was the nickname many people gave to the type of workhouse introduced by the Poor Law Amendment Act of 1834.

Chartism a working-class movement which said that Parliament should accept the six demands of the **People's Charter**. Supporters of Chartism were called **Chartists**. They believed that working people should be able to become MPs so they could argue for laws which would benefit the workers.

Complete Suffrage Union formed in 1842 by Joseph Sturge and William Lovett. The Union said that the working class should join with the middle class and campaign for all people to be given the right to vote.

Corn Laws reintroduced by the government in 1815. Foreign corn was banned from Britain, unless the price of British corn was £4 per quarter or over. This kept the price of corn (and therefore bread) much higher than it should have been.

London Working Men's Association formed in 1836 and made up of skilled craftsmen. Its secretary was William Lovett. Members of the LWMA wrote the six points of the People's Charter.

Methodists a religious group formed by John Wesley in 1729. The Methodists broke away from the Church of England in 1795. Many working-class people supported the Methodist church in the nineteenth century.

National Chartist Association an organization set up in 1840 to spread the ideas of Chartism. It had branches throughout the country.

Poor Law Amendment Act passed in 1834. It brought in the New Poor Law. Parishes had to join together into Poor Law Unions and provide a workhouse.

Poor Law Commissioners were appointed to go round checking that the workhouses were being properly run.

Radicals people who believed strongly that everyone should have the right to vote.

Reform Act (1832) gave the middle class the right to vote. Also gave MPs to the growing industrial towns of the north.

Six Acts passed in 1819 after the Peterloo Massacre. The Acts were designed to stop large meetings taking place.

Tory Party in the early 1800s was made up of landowners and farmers. The Tories did not favour giving the vote to the working class.

Whig Party in the early 1800s was supported by middle-class people. The Whigs thought that Parliament should be changed – but not too much.

Index